A Book of Devotions

Large Print Edition

Compiled by
Joseph Coppolino

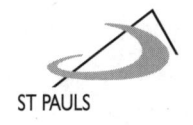

ST PAULS

Alba House

Nihil Obstat:
James T. O'Connor, STD
Censor Librorum

Imprimatur:
✠ Joseph T. O'Keefe, DD
Vicar General, Archdiocese of New York
December 20, 1985

The Nihil Obstat and Imprimatur are official declarations
that a book or pamphlet is free of doctrinal or moral
error. No implication is contained therein that those
who have granted the Nihil Obstat and Imprimatur agree
with the contents, opinions or statements expressed.

Produced and designed in the United States of America by the
Fathers and Brothers of the Society of St. Paul,
2187 Victory Boulevard, Staten Island, New York 10314-6603,
as part of their communications apostolate.

Printing Information:

Current Printing - first digit	4	5	6	7	8	9	10

Year of Current Printing - first year shown

2005	2006	2007	2008	2009	2010	2011	2012

Contents

Act of Consecration to the Immaculate Heart of Mary 5
Morning Offering 6
Blue Army Pledge 6
Formula of The Heroic Act 7
Angel Prayer 8
Eucharist Prayer 8
Rosary Decade Prayer 8
Pardon Prayer 9
Sacrifice Prayer 9
Prayer of Mercy 9
Prayer to our Blessed Mother 10
The Fifteen Prayers as revealed by Our Lord
    to Saint Bridget 11
Salutation of the Wound in the Shoulder of Jesus 23
Invocations in honor of the Holy Wounds of
    Our Lord Jesus Christ 24
Prayer to Jesus Crucified 24
Anima Christi 25
To Our Lord on the Cross 25
Act of Consecration to the Sacred Heart of Jesus 26
Veni, Creator 27
Magnificat 28
Ave, Maris Stella 29
Litany of the Holy Spirit 31
Litany of the Blessed Virgin 34
Litany of the Holy Name of Jesus 37
Litany of the Sacred Heart of Jesus 41
Litany of Saint Joseph 44
Prayers to Saint Joseph 47
Prayer from The Little Office of the Immaculate
    Conception of the Blessed Virgin Mary 52
The New Secret of Salvation 65
Perpetual Novena in honor of Our Lady
    of the Miraculous Medal 71

Act of Consecration to the Immaculate Heart of Mary

(St. Louis de Montfort's Consecration)

I, N., a faithless sinner—renew and ratify today in thy hands, O Immaculate Mother, the vows of my Baptism; I renounce forever Satan, his pomps and works; and I give myself entirely to Jesus Christ, the Incarnate Wisdom, to carry my cross after Him all the days of my life, and to be more faithful to Him than I have ever been before.

In the presence of all the heavenly court I choose thee this day for my Mother and Mistress. I deliver and consecrate to thee, as thy slave, my body and soul, my goods, both interior and exterior, and even the value of all my good actions, past, present and future; leaving to thee the entire and full right of disposing of me, and all that belongs to me, without exception, according to thy good pleasure, for the greater glory of God, in time and in eternity. Amen.

Morning Offering

O my Jesus, through the Immaculate Heart of Mary I offer Thee all my prayers, works, joys and sufferings of this day. In union with the Holy Sacrifice of the Mass throughout the world. In reparation for all my sins, for the intention of our Holy Father the Pope, the poor souls in Purgatory, the conversion of sinners, and the reign of Thy Sacred Heart and the Immaculate Heart of Mary throughout the world. Amen.

Blue Army Pledge

O my God, in union with the Immaculate Heart of Mary (here kiss your Brown Scapular as a sign of your consecration), I offer Thee the precious Blood of Jesus united with His most Sacred Wounds from all the altars throughout the world, joining with It the offering of my every thought, word and action of this day. Amen.

O my Jesus, I desire today to gain every indulgence and merit I can, united with Thy most Sacred Wounds and I offer them, together with myself, to Mary Immaculate, that she may best apply them to the interest of Thy most Sacred Heart. Precious Blood of Jesus, save us! Immaculate Heart of Mary, pray for us! Sacred Heart of Jesus, have mercy on us! Amen.

Formula of The Heroic Act

O Holy and Adorable Trinity, desiring to cooperate in the deliverance of the souls in purgatory, and to testify my devotion to the Blessed Virgin Mary, I cede and renounce in behalf of those holy souls all the satisfactory part of my works, and all the suffrages which may be given to me after my death, consigning them entirely into the hands of the most Blessed Virgin Mary, that she may apply them according to her good pleasure to those souls of the faithful departed whom she desires to deliver from their sufferings. Deign, O my God, to accept and bless this offering which I make to Thee at this moment. Amen.

Angel Prayer

O Most Holy Trinity, Father, Son, and Holy Spirit, I adore Thee profoundly. I offer Thee the Most Precious Body, Blood, Soul and Divinity of Jesus Christ, present in all the tabernacles of the world, in reparation for the outrages, sacrileges and indifference by which He is offended. By the infinite merits of the Sacred Heart of Jesus and the Immaculate Heart of Mary, I beg the conversion of poor sinners. Amen.

Eucharist Prayer

Most Holy Trinity, I adore Thee! My God, my God, I love Thee in the Most Blessed Sacrament. Amen.

Rosary Decade Prayer

O my Jesus, forgive us our sins, save us from the fires of hell, lead all souls to heaven, especially those in most need of Thy Mercy. Amen.

Jesus, Mary and Joseph, I love You, save souls. Amen.

Pardon Prayer

My God, I believe, I adore, I trust and I love Thee! I beg pardon for those who do not believe, do not adore, do not trust and do not love Thee. Amen.

Sacrifice Prayer

O my Jesus, it is for love of You, in reparation for the offenses committed against the Immaculate Heart of Mary, and for the conversion of poor sinners. Amen.

Prayer of Mercy

Behold, O my God, the traitor who has so often rebelled against You. Alas! I am filled with regret; I abhor and detest with all my heart my innumerable sins. I offer You in expiation the same satisfaction which Jesus Christ offers on the altar; His merits, His blood, and Himself, God Incarnate, Who, as Victim, deigns to renew His Sacrifice daily on our altars for our sake. As my Jesus is Himself my Mediator and Advocate on the altar, and is asking You to have mercy on me through His Precious Blood, I join my voice to His adorable pleading, and ask Your forgiveness for the enormity of my sins. O God of my heart, if my tears do not touch You, listen to the groanings of Jesus, and as He obtained mercy on the Cross for the whole world, may He obtain it for me on the altar! I humbly trust that through the merits of His Precious Blood You will forgive me all my sins, which I shall bewail to my last breath. My beloved Jesus, give me the tears of St. Peter, the contrition of Mary Magdalen, and the sorrow of all the saints, who from sinners became true penitents, that I may obtain complete forgiveness of my sins through the Holy Sacrifice of the Mass. Amen.

Prayer to our Blessed Mother

O Mary, O Mother, most afflicted of all mothers! I compassionate thy Heart, more especially when thou didst behold thy Jesus surrender Himself on the Cross, open His mouth, and expire; and, for love of this thy

Son, now dead for my salvation, do thou recommend unto Him my soul. And do Thou, my Jesus, for the sake of the merits of Mary's sorrows, have mercy upon me, and grant me the grace of dying for Thee, as Thou hast died for me; "May I die, O my Lord, (will I say unto Thee, with St. Francis of Assisi), for love of the love of Thee, Who hast vouchsafed to die for love of the love of me." Amen.

The Fifteen Prayers as revealed by Our Lord to Saint Bridget

1st Prayer—Our Father, Hail Mary...

O Jesus Christ! Eternal sweetness to those who love Thee, joy surpassing all joy and all desire, salvation and hope of all sinners; Thou who hast proved that Thou hast no greater desire than to be amongst men even assuming human nature during the course of time for love of men, recall all the sufferings that Thou hast endured from the first moment of Thy conception, and especially during Thy passion, as it was decreed and ordained from all eternity in the Divine plan.

Remember, O Lord, that during the Last Supper with Thy disciples, having washed their feet, Thou gavest them Thy Precious Body and Blood, and while at the same time Thou didst sweetly console them, Thou didst foretell them Thy coming Passion.

Remember the sadness and bitterness which Thou didst experience in Thy soul as Thou prayed: "My soul is sorrowful even unto death."

Remember all the fear, anguish and pain that Thou didst suffer in Thy delicate Body before the crucifixion, when, after having prayed three separate times, bathed in a "sweat of blood," Thou wast betrayed by Judas, Thy disciple, arrested by the people of a nation Thou hadst chosen and elevated, accused by false witnesses, unjustly judged by three judges, all this in the flower of Thy youth and during the solemn Paschal season.

Remember that Thou wast despoiled of Thy garments and clothed with the garments of derision; that Thy face and eyes were veiled, that Thou wast buffeted, crowned with thorns, a scepter placed in Thy hands, that Thou wast fastened to a column and crushed with blows and overwhelmed with affronts and outrages.

In memory of all these pains and sufferings which Thou didst endure before Thy Passion on the Cross, grant that before I die, I may with true contrition make a sincere and entire confession, make worthy satisfaction and be granted the remission of all my sins. Amen.

2nd Prayer—Our Father, Hail Mary...

O Jesus! True Liberty of angels, Paradise of delights, remember the horror and sadness which Thou didst endure when Thy enemies, like furious lions, surrounded Thee, and by thousands of blows, insults, lacerations, and other unheard of cruelties, tormented Thee at will.

Through these torments and insulting words, I beg of Thee, O my Savior, to deliver me from all enemies, both visible and invisible, that under Thy protection, I may attain the perfection of eternal salvation. Amen.

3rd Prayer—Our Father, Hail Mary…

O Jesus! Creator of heaven and earth, Whom nothing can encompass nor limit, Thou Who dost enfold and hold all under Thy loving power, remember the very bitter pain which Thou didst suffer when blow by blow and with hatred the Jews nailed Thy sacred hands and feet to the Cross, with big blunt nails, and, not finding Thee in a pitiable enough state to satisfy their rage, they enlarged Thy wounds, and added pain to pain, and with indescribable cruelty stretched Thy Body on the Cross, and dislocated Thy bones by pulling them on all sides.

I beg of Thee, O Jesus, by the memory of this most holy and most loving suffering of the Cross, to grant me the grace to fear Thee and love Thee. Amen.

4th Prayer—Our Father, Hail Mary…

O Jesus! Heavenly Physician raised aloft on the Cross in order that through Thy Wounds, ours might be healed; remember the bruises which Thou didst suffer and the weakness of all Thy members which were stretched to such a degree that never was there pain like unto Thine; from the crown of Thy head to the soles of Thy feet there was not one spot of Thy Body that was not in torment; and yet, forgetting all Thy sufferings, Thou didst not cease to pray to Thy Heavenly Father for Thy enemies, saying, "Father, forgive them, they know not what they do."

Through this great mercy, and in memory of this suffering, grant that the remembrance of Thy most bitter Passion my effect in us a perfect contrition and the remission of all our sins. Amen.

5th Prayer—Our Father, Hail Mary…

O Jesus! Mirror of eternal splendor, remember the sadness which Thou experienced, when, contemplating in the light of Thy Divinity the predestination of those who would be saved by the merits of Thy Sacred Passion, Thou didst see at the same time the great multitude of reprobates who would be damned for their sins, and Thou didst complain bitterly of those hopeless, lost and unfortunate sinners.

Through this abyss of compassion and pity, and especially through the goodness which Thou displayed to the good thief when Thou said to him: "This day thou shalt be with Me in Paradise." I beg of Thee, O sweet Jesus, that at the hour of my death Thou wilt show me mercy. Amen.

6th Prayer—Our Father, Hail Mary...

O Jesus! King most loving and most desirable, remember the grief which Thou didst suffer, when naked and like a common criminal, Thou wast raised and fastened to the Cross, when all Thy relatives and friends abandoned Thee, except Thy beloved Mother who remained close to Thee during Thy agony and whom Thou didst entrust to Thy faithful disciple when Thou saidst to Mary: "Woman, behold thy son," and to St. John: "Behold thy Mother."

I beg of Thee, O my Savior, by the sword of sorrow which pierced the soul of Thy holy Mother, to have compassion on me in all my afflictions and tribulations, both corporal and spiritual and to assist me in all my trials, and especially at the hour of my death. Amen.

7th Prayer—Our Father, Hail Mary…

O Jesus! Inexhaustible fountain of compassion, Who by a profound gesture of love, said from the Cross: "I thirst!" suffered from the thirst for the salvation of the human race, I beg of Thee, O my Savior, to inflame in our hearts the desire to tend toward perfection in all of our acts; and to extinguish in us the concupiscence of the flesh and the ardor of worldly desires. Amen.

8th Prayer—Our Father, Hail Mary…

O Jesus! Sweetness of hearts, delight of the spirit, by the bitterness of the gall and the vinegar which Thou didst taste on the Cross for the love of us, grant us the grace to receive worthily Thy Precious Body and Blood during our life and at the hour of our death, that it may serve us as a remedy and consolation for our souls. Amen.

9th Prayer—Our Father, Hail Mary…

O Jesus! Royal virtue and mental delight, recall the anguish and pain which Thou didst endure, when, from the bitterness of agonizing death and the insults of Thy persecutors, Thou didst exclaim in a loud voice that Thou wast forsaken by the Father, saying: "My God, My God, why hast Thou forsaken Me?"

Through this anguish, I beg of Thee, O my Savior, not to abandon me during the anguish and pains of my death. Amen.

10th Prayer—Our Father, Hail Mary…

O Jesus! Thou Who art the beginning and the end of all things, life and virtue, remember that for our sakes Thou wast plunged into an abyss of suffering from the soles of Thy feet to the crown of Thy head. In consideration of the enormity of Thy wounds, teach me to keep, through pure love, Thy Commandments, Whose way is wide and easy for those who love Thee. Amen.

11th Prayer—Our Father, Hail Mary…

O Jesus! Deep abyss of mercy, I beg of Thee, in memory of Thy wounds which penetrated to the very marrow of Thy bones and to the depth of Thy being, to draw me, a miserable sinner, overwhelmed by my offenses, away from sin and to hide me from Thy face, justly irritated against me. Hide me in Thy wounds until Thy anger and indignation shall have passed away. Amen.

12th Prayer—Our Father, Hail Mary…

O Jesus! Mirror of Truth, symbol of unity, bond of charity, remember the multitude of wounds with which Thou wast afflicted from head to foot, torn and reddened by the spilling of Thy adorable Blood, O great and universal pain, which Thou didst suffer in Thy virginal flesh for love of us! Sweetest Jesus! What is there that Thou couldst have done for us which Thou hast not done!

May the fruit of Thy suffering be renewed in my soul by the faithful remembrance of Thy Passion, and may Thy love increase in my heart each day, until I see Thee in eternity; Thou Who art the treasure of every real good and every joy, which I beg Thee to grant me, O Sweetest Jesus, in heaven. Amen.

13th Prayer—Our Father, Hail Mary...

O Jesus! Strong Lion, Immortal and Invincible King, remember the pain which Thou didst endure when all Thy strength, moral and physical, was entirely exhausted, Thou didst bow Thy head saying: "All is consummated!"

Through this anguish and grief, I beg of Thee, O Lord, to have mercy on me at the hour of my death, when my mind will be greatly troubled and my soul will be in anguish. Amen.

14th Prayer—Our Father, Hail Mary...

O Jesus! Only-Begotten Son of the Father, Splendor and Figure of His Substance, remember the simple and humble recommendation Thou didst make of Thy soul to the Eternal Father, saying: "Father, into Thy hands I commend My Spirit"; and when Thy Body, all torn, and Thy Heart, broken, and the bowels of Thy mercy open to redeem us, Thou didst expire. Through this precious death, I beg Thee, O King of Saints, comfort me and give me help to resist the devil, the flesh, and the world so that, being dead to the world, I may live for Thee alone. I beg of Thee at the hour of my death to receive me, a pilgrim and an exile returning to Thee. Amen.

15th Prayer—Our Father, Hail Mary...

O Jesus! True and fruitful Vine! Remember the abundant outpouring of Blood which Thou didst so generously shed from Thy Sacred Body as juice from grapes in a wine press.

From Thy side, pierced with the lance by

a soldier, blood and water issued forth until there was not left in Thy Body a single drop, and finally, like a bundle of myrrh lifted to the very top of the Cross, Thy delicate flesh was destroyed, the very substance of Thy Body withered, and the marrow of Thy bones dried up.

Through this bitter Passion and through the outpouring of Thy Precious Blood, I beg of Thee, O Sweet Jesus, to receive my soul when I am in my death agony. Amen.

Oh Sweet Jesus! Pierce my heart so that my tears of penitence and love will be my bread day and night; may I be converted entirely to Thee; may my heart be Thy perpetual habitation, may my conversation be pleasing to Thee, and may the end of my life be so praiseworthy that I may merit heaven, and there, with Thy saints, praise Thee forever and ever. Amen.

Our Father, Hail Mary, Glory be — 3 times

Salutation of the Wound in the Shoulder of Jesus

O most loving Jesus, meekest Lamb of God, I, a miserable sinner, salute and worship the most Sacred Wound of Thy Shoulder on which Thou didst bear Thy heavy Cross, which so tore Thy flesh and laid bare Thy bones as to inflict on Thee an anguish greater than any other wound of Thy most Blessed Body. I adore Thee, O Jesus most sorrowful. I praise Thee, I bless Thee and glorify Thee and give Thee thanks for this most sacred and most painful Wound. Beseeching Thee by that exceeding pain, and the crushing burden of Thy heavy Cross, to be merciful to me, a sinner, to forgive me all my mortal and venial sins, and to lead me on towards Heaven along the way of the Cross. Amen.

Invocations in honor of the Holy Wounds of Our Lord Jesus Christ

On the large beads:

Eternal Father, I offer Thee the Wounds of Our Lord Jesus Christ to heal the wounds of our souls. Amen.

On the small beads:

My Jesus, pardon and mercy through the merits of Thy Sacred Wounds. Amen.

Prayer to Jesus Crucified

Look down upon me, good and gentle Jesus, while before Thy face, I humbly kneel, and with burning soul pray and beseech Thee to fix deep in my heart lively sentiments of faith, hope and charity, true contrition for my sins, and a firm purpose of amendment; while I contemplate with love and tender pity Thy five wounds, pondering over them within me, and calling to mind what the prophet David put in Thy mouth concerning Thee, O good Jesus: "They have pierced my hands and my feet; they have numbered all my bones." Amen.

Anima Christi

Soul of Christ, sanctify me.
Body of Christ, save me.
Blood of Christ, inebriate me.
Water from the side of Christ, wash me.
O good Jesus, hear me.
Within Thy Wounds hide me.
Permit me not to be separated from Thee.
From the malignant enemy defend me.
In the hour of my death, call me,
And bid me come to Thee,
That with Thy saints, I may praise Thee
Forever and ever. Amen.

To Our Lord on the Cross

My Crucified Jesus, mercifully accept the prayer which I now make to Thee for help in the moment of my death, when at its approach, all my senses shall fail me. When, therefore, O sweetest Jesus, my weary and downcast eyes can no longer look up to Thee, be mindful of the loving gaze which I now turn on Thee, and have mercy on me. When my parched lips can no longer kiss Thy most sacred wounds, remember then those kisses which now I imprint on Thee, and have mercy on me. When my cold hands can no longer embrace Thy Cross, forget not the affection with which I embrace it now, and have mercy on me. And when at length, my swollen and lifeless tongue can no longer speak, remember that I called upon Thee now. Jesus, Mary, Joseph, to you I commend my soul. Jesus, Mary, Joseph, I love You. Save souls! Amen.

Act of Consecration to the Sacred Heart of Jesus

O amiable Heart of my Savior, I adore Thee!
O gracious Heart of Jesus, I love Thee!
O compassionate Heart, I give Thee my heart, and am deeply moved by all Thou hast done and suffered for me.
Yes, I give Thee my whole heart; attach it eternally to Thyself, inflame it with Thy love, inspire it with Thy sentiments, make it know Thy Will and practice Thy virtues. Amen.

Veni, Creator

Come, O Creator Spirit Blest!
And in our souls take up Thy rest;
Come with Thy grace and heavenly aid,
To fill the hearts which Thou hast made.

Great Paraclete! To Thee we cry,
O highest gift of God most high!
O font of life! O fire of love!
And sweet anointing from above.

Thou in Thy sevenfold gifts are known,
The finger of God's hand we own;
The promise of the Father, Thou!
Who dost the tongue with power endow.

Kindle our senses from above.
And make our hearts o'erflow with love;
With patience firm and virtue high
The weakness of our flesh supply.

Far from us drive the foe we dread,
And grant us Thy true peace instead;
So shall we not, with Thee for guide,
Turn from the path of life aside.

Oh, may Thy grace on us bestow
The Father, and the Son to know,

And Thee through endless times confessed
Of both the eternal Spirit blest.

All glory while the ages run
Be to the Father and the Son
Who rose from death; the same to Thee,
O Holy Spirit, eternally. Amen.

Magnificat

My soul doth magnify the Lord.

And my spirit hath rejoiced in God my Savior.

Because He hath regarded the humility of His handmaid; for behold, from henceforth all generations shall call me blessed.

Because He that is mighty hath done great things to me; and holy is His name.

And His mercy is from generation to generation, to them that fear Him.

He hath showed might in His arm; He hath scattered the proud in the conceit of their heart.

He hath put down the mighty from their seat; and hath exalted the humble.

He hath filled the hungry with good things; and the rich he hath sent empty away.

He hath received Israel His servant, being mindful of His mercy.

As He spoke to our fathers, to Abraham and to his seed forever. Amen.

Glory be to the Father, etc.

Ave, Maris Stella

Hail, bright star of ocean,
God's own Mother blest,
Ever sinless Virgin,
Gate of heavenly rest.

Taking that sweet Ave
Which from Gabriel came,
Peace confirm within us,
Changing Eva's name.

Break the captives' fetters,
Light of blindness pour,

All our ills expelling,
Every bliss implore.

Show thyself a Mother;
May the Word Divine,
Born for us thy Infant,
Hear our prayers through thine.

Virgin all excelling,
Mildest of the mild,
Freed from guilt, preserve us,
Pure and undefiled.

Keep our life all spotless
Make our way secure,
Till we find in Jesus
Joy forevermore.

Through the highest Heaven
To the Almighty Three,
Father, Son and Spirit,
One same glory be. Amen.

Litany of the Holy Spirit

Lord, have mercy on us.
Christ, have mercy on us.
Lord, have mercy on us.
Father all powerful, *have mercy on us.*
Jesus, Eternal Son of the Father,
Redeemer of the world, *save us.*
Spirit of the Father and the Son,
boundless life of both, *sanctify us.*
Holy Trinity, *hear us.*
Holy Spirit, Who proceedest from the
Father and the Son, *enter our hearts.*
Holy Spirit, Who art equal to the Father
and the Son, *enter our hearts.*

Promise of God the Father,
Ray of heavenly light,
Author of all good,
Source of heavenly water,
Consuming fire,
Spiritual unction,
Spirit of love and truth,
Spirit of wisdom and understanding,
Spirit of counsel and fortitude,
Spirit of knowledge and piety,
Spirit of the fear of the Lord,

Have mercy on us

Spirit of grace and prayer,
Spirit of peace and meekness,
Spirit of modesty and innocence,
Holy Spirit, the Comforter,
Holy Spirit, the Sanctifier,
Holy Spirit, Who governest the Church,
Gift of God, the Most High,
Spirit Who fillest the universe,
Spirit of the adoption of the children of God,

Have mercy on us

Holy Spirit, *inspire us with horror of sin.*
Holy Spirit, *come and renew the face of the earth.*
Holy Spirit, *shed Thy light in our souls.*
Holy Spirit, *engrave Thy law in our hearts.*
Holy Spirit, *inflame us with the flame of Thy love.*
Holy Spirit, *open to us the treasures of Thy graces.*
Holy Spirit, *teach us to pray well.*
Holy Spirit, *enlighten us with Thy heavenly inspirations.*
Holy Spirit, *lead us in the way of salvation.*
Holy Spirit, *grant us the only necessary knowledge.*

Holy Spirit, *inspire in us the practice of good.*
Holy Spirit, *grant us the merits of all virtues.*
Holy Spirit, *make us persevere in justice.*
Holy Spirit, *be Thou our everlasting reward.*
Lamb of God, Who takes away the sins of the world, *send us Thy Holy Spirit.*
Lamb of God, Who takes away the sins of the world, *pour down into our souls the gifts of the Holy Spirit.*
Lamb of God, Who takes away the sins of the world, *grant us the Spirit of wisdom and piety.*

V. Come, Holy Spirit! Fill the hearts of Thy faithful.
R. And enkindle in them the fire of Thy love.

Let us Pray

Grant, O merciful Father, that Thy Divine Spirit enlighten, inflame and purify us, that He may penetrate us with His heavenly dew and make us fruitful in good works; through our Lord Jesus Christ, Thy Son, Who with Thee, in the unity of the same Spirit, lives and reigns forever and ever. Amen.

Litany of the Blessed Virgin

Lord, have mercy on us.
Christ, have mercy on us.
Lord, have mercy on us.
Christ, hear us.
Christ, graciously hear us.
God the Father of heaven, *have mercy on us.*
God the Son, Redeemer of the world, *have mercy on us.*
God the Holy Spirit, *have mercy on us.*
Holy Trinity, one God, *have mercy on us.*
Holy Mary, *pray for us.*
Holy Mother of God,
Holy Virgin of virgins,
Mother of Christ,
Mother of divine grace,
Mother most pure,
Mother most chaste,
Mother inviolate,
Mother undefiled,
Mother most amiable,
Mother most admirable,
Mother of good counsel,
Mother of our Creator,
Mother of our Savior,

Pray for us

Mother of the Church,
Virgin most prudent,
Virgin most venerable,
Virgin most renowned,
Virgin most powerful,
Virgin most merciful,
Virgin most faithful,
Mirror of justice,
Seat of wisdom,
Cause of our joy,
Spiritual vessel,
Vessel of honor,
Singular vessel of devotion,
Mystical rose,
Tower of David,
Tower of ivory,
House of gold,
Ark of the covenant,
Gate of Heaven,
Morning star,
Health of the sick,
Refuge of sinners,
Comforter of the afflicted,
Help of Christians,
Queen of angels,

Pray for us

Queen of patriarchs,
Queen of prophets,
Queen of Apostles,
Queen of martyrs,
Queen of confessors,
Queen of virgins,
Queen of all saints,
Queen conceived without original sin,
Queen of the most holy Rosary,
Queen assumed into Heaven,
Queen of peace,

Pray for us

Lamb of God, Who takes away the sins of the world, *spare us O Lord.*

Lamb of God, Who takes away the sins of the world, *graciously hear us, O Lord.*

Lamb of God, Who takes away the sins of the world, *have mercy on us.*

Christ hear us,
Christ graciously hear us.

V. Pray for us, O holy Mother of God.
R. That we may be made worthy of the promises of Christ.

Let us Pray

Grant unto us, Thy servants, we beseech Thee, O Lord God, at all times to enjoy health of soul and body; and by the glorious intercession of Blessed Mary, ever virgin, when freed from the sorrows of this present life, to enter into that joy which has no end. Through Christ our Lord. Amen.

Litany of the Holy Name of Jesus

Lord, have mercy on us.
Christ, have mercy on us.
Lord, have mercy on us.
Jesus, hear us.
Jesus, graciously hear us.
God the Father of heaven,
God the Son, Redeemer of the world,
God the Holy Spirit,
Holy Trinity, one God,
Jesus, Son of the living God,
Jesus, splendor of the Father,
Jesus, brightness of eternal light,
Jesus, King of glory,

Have mercy on us

Jesus, sun of justice,
Jesus, son of the Virgin Mary,
Jesus, most amiable,
Jesus, most admirable,
Jesus, mighty God,
Jesus, Father of the world to come,
Jesus, angel of the great council,
Jesus, most powerful,
Jesus, most patient,
Jesus, most obedient,
Jesus, meek and humble of heart,
Jesus, lover of chastity,
Jesus, lover of us,
Jesus, God of peace,
Jesus, author of life,
Jesus, model of virtues,
Jesus, lover of souls,
Jesus, our God,
Jesus, our refuge,
Jesus, Father of the poor,
Jesus, treasure of the faithful,
Jesus, Good Shepherd,
Jesus, true light,
Jesus, eternal wisdom,
Jesus, infinite goodness,

Have mercy on us

Jesus, our way and our life,
Jesus, joy of angels,
Jesus, king of Patriarchs,
Jesus, master of Apostles,
Jesus, teacher of Evangelists,
Jesus, strength of martyrs,
Jesus, light of confessors,
Jesus, purity of virgins,
Jesus, crown of all saints, *Have mercy on us*

Be merciful, *spare us, O Jesus.*
Be merciful, *graciously hear us, O Jesus.*

From all evil,
From all sin,
From Thy wrath,
From the snares of the devil,
From the spirit of fornication,
From everlasting death,
From the neglect of Thine inspirations,
Through the mystery of Thy holy Incarnation,
Through Thy nativity,
Through Thine infancy,
Through Thy most divine life,
Through Thy labors,
Through Thine agony and Passion, *Jesus, deliver us*

Through Thy cross and dereliction,
Through Thy sufferings,
Through Thy death and burial,
Through Thy Resurrection,
Through Thine Ascension,
Through Thine institution of the most Holy Eucharist,
Through Thy joys,
Through Thy glory,

Jesus, deliver us

Lamb of God, Who takes away the sins of the world, *spare us O Jesus.*

Lamb of God, Who takes away the sins of the world, *graciously hear us, O Jesus.*

Lamb of God, Who takes away the sins of the world, *have mercy on us.*

Jesus hear us.
Jesus, graciously hear us.

Let us Pray

O Lord, Jesus Christ, Who has said: Ask and you shall receive; seek and you shall find; knock and it shall be opened unto you: grant, we beseech Thee, to us who ask the gift of Thy divine love, that we may ever love Thee with all our hearts, and in all our words and actions, and never cease praising Thee.

Give us O Lord, a perpetual fear and love of Thy holy Name; for Thou never failest to govern those whom Thou dost solidly establish in Thy love. Who livest and reignest world without end. Amen.

Litany of the Sacred Heart of Jesus

Lord, have mercy on us.
Christ, have mercy on us.
Lord, have mercy on us.
Christ, hear us.
Christ, graciously hear us.
God the Father of Heaven,
God the Son, Redeemer of the world,
God the Holy Spirit,
Holy Trinity, one God,
Heart of Jesus, Son of the
   Eternal Father,
Heart of Jesus, formed by the
   Holy Spirit in the womb of
   the Virgin Mother,
Heart of Jesus, substantially united
   with the Word of God,

Have mercy on us

Heart of Jesus, of infinite majesty,
Heart of Jesus, holy temple of God,
Heart of Jesus, house of God and gate of Heaven,
Heart of Jesus, burning furnace of charity,
Heart of Jesus, abode of justice and love,
Heart of Jesus, full of goodness and love,
Heart of Jesus, abyss of all virtues,
Heart of Jesus, most worthy of all praise,
Heart of Jesus, King and center of all hearts,
Heart of Jesus, in whom are all the treasures of wisdom and knowledge,
Heart of Jesus, in whom dwells all the fullness of divinity,
Heart of Jesus, in whom the Father was well pleased,
Heart of Jesus, of whose fullness we have all received,
Heart of Jesus, desire of the everlasting hills,
Heart of Jesus, patient and most merciful,
Heart of Jesus, enriching all who invoke Thee,

Have mercy on us

Heart of Jesus, fountain of life
and holiness,
Heart of Jesus, propitiation for our sins,
Heart of Jesus, loaded down with
opprobrium,
Heart of Jesus, bruised for our offenses,
Heart of Jesus, obedient unto death,
Heart of Jesus, pierced with a lance,
Heart of Jesus, source of all consolation,
Heart of Jesus, our life and resurrection,
Heart of Jesus, our peace and
reconciliation,
Heart of Jesus, victim for sin,
Heart of Jesus, salvation of those
who trust in Thee,
Heart of Jesus, delight of all the saints,

Have mercy on us

Lamb of God, Who takes away the sins of the world, *spare us O Lord.*

Lamb of God, Who takes away the sins of the world, *graciously hear us, O Lord.*

Lamb of God, Who takes away the sins of the world, *have mercy on us.*

V. Jesus meek and humble of heart.
R. Make our hearts like unto Thine.

Let us Pray

Almighty and everlasting God, graciously regard the heart of Thy well-beloved Son and the acts of praise and satisfaction which He renders Thee on behalf of us sinners, and through their merit grant pardon to us who implore Thy mercy, in the name of Thy Son Jesus Christ; Who liveth and reigneth with Thee in the unity of the Holy Spirit, one God world without end. Amen.

Litany of Saint Joseph

Lord, have mercy on us.
Christ, have mercy on us.
Lord, have mercy on us.
Christ, hear us.
Christ, graciously hear us.
God the Father of heaven, *have mercy on us.*
God the Son, Redeemer of the world, *have mercy on us.*
God the Holy Spirit, *have mercy on us.*
Holy Trinity, one God, *have mercy on us.*
Holy Mary, *pray for us.*

St. Joseph,
Illustrious Son of David,
Light of the Patriarchs,
Spouse of the Mother of God,
Chaste Guardian of the Virgin,
Foster-Father of the Son of God,
Watchful Defender of Christ,
Head of the Holy Family,
Joseph most just,
Joseph most chaste,
Joseph most prudent,
Joseph most valiant,
Joseph most obedient,
Joseph most faithful,
Mirror of patience,
Lover of poverty,
Model of workmen,
Glory of domestic life,
Guardian of virgins,
Pillar of families,
Solace of the afflicted,
Hope of the sick,
Patron of the dying,
Terror of demons,
Protector of Holy Church.

Pray for us

Lamb of God, Who takes away the sins of the world, *spare us O Lord.*

Lamb of God, Who takes away the sins of the world, *graciously hear us, O Lord.*

Lamb of God, Who takes away the sins of the world, *have mercy on us.*

V. He made him the lord of His house.
R. And the ruler of all His possessions.

Let us Pray

O God, Who in Your unspeakable providence did choose Blessed Joseph to be the spouse of Your most Holy Mother, grant that as we venerate him as our protector on earth, we may deserve to have him as our intercessor in heaven through our Lord Jesus Christ, Thy Son. Amen.

Prayer to Saint Joseph

To you, blessed Joseph, we come with confidence in this hour of need, trusting in your powerful protection. Your loving service to the Immaculate Virgin Mother of God and your fatherly affection for the Child Jesus inspire us with faith in the power of your intercession before the throne of God.

We pray, first of all, for the Church: that it may be free from error and corruption, and be a shining light of universal love and justice.

We ask your intercession for our loved ones in their trials and adversities, that they may be inspired by the love, obedience and affection of the Holy Family, and be to each other a mutual source of consolation and Christian fidelity.

We ask your intercession also for our special need (here mention the grace desired).

Keep us one and all under your protection so that, strengthened by your example and assistance, we may lead a holy life, die a happy death, and come to the possession of everlasting happiness in heaven. Amen.

Let us Pray

Assist us, Lord, by the merits of Your foster father, St. Joseph, spouse of Your most Holy Mother. May his help gain for us what our own efforts cannot obtain. This we ask through You Who live and reign with God the Father in the union of the Holy Spirit, one God, for all the ages. Amen.

Saint Joseph, Patron of Workers

Blessed St. Joseph, patron of all working people, obtain for me the grace to labor in a spirit of penance for the atonement of my many sins. Help me to be conscientious in my work so that I may give as full a measure as I have received.

May I labor in a spirit of thankfulness and joy, ever mindful of all the gifts I have received from God that enable me to perform these tasks. Permit me to work in peace, patience and moderation, keeping in mind the account I must one day give of time lost, talents unused, good omitted and vanity of success, so fatal to the work of God. Glorious St. Joseph, may my labors be all for Jesus, all through Mary and all after your holy example in life and in death. Amen.

Prayer to Saint Joseph

O Holy Joseph, chaste spouse of the Mother of God, most glorious advocate of all who are in danger or in their last agony, and most faithful protector of all the servants of Mary, I, N., in the presence of Jesus and Mary, do from this moment choose you for my powerful patron and advocate, and I implore you to obtain for me through your powerful intercession the grace of a happy death.

Receive me, therefore, for your perpetual servant, and recommend me to the constant protection of Mary, your spouse, and to the everlasting mercies of Jesus my Savior.

Assist me in all the actions of my life, which I now offer to the greater glory of Jesus and Mary.

Never, therefore, forsake me; and whatsoever grace you see most necessary and profitable for me, obtain it for me now and also at the hour of my death.

Through your gracious intercession may there be granted me in my last hour all the graces I need, through the merits of Jesus Christ, my Savior, Who together with the Father and the Holy Spirit, lives and reigns, world without end. Amen.

Prayer for Virginity

O Blessed Saint Joseph, faithful guardian and protector of virgins, to whom God entrusted Jesus and Mary, I implore you by the love which you did bear them, to preserve me from every defilement of soul and body, that I may always serve them in holiness and purity of love. Amen.

Prayer for Purity

Saint Joseph, father and guardian of virgins, into whose faithful keeping were entrusted Innocence itself, I pray and beseech you through Jesus and Mary, those pledges so dear to you, to keep me from all uncleanness, and to grant that my mind may be untainted, my heart pure, and my body chaste.

Help me always to serve Jesus and Mary in perfect chastity. Amen.

For a Happy Death

O Blessed St. Joseph, who died in the arms of Jesus and Mary, obtain for me, I beseech you, the grace of a happy death. In that hour of dread and anguish, assist me by your power against the enemies of my salvation. Into your hands, living and dying, Jesus, Mary and Joseph, I commend my soul. Amen.

O Jesus Living In Mary

O Jesus living in Mary,
Come and live in Thy servants,
In the spirit of Thy holiness,
In the fullness of Thy might,
In the truth of Thy virtues,
In the perfection of Thy ways,
In the communion of Thy mysteries,
Subdue every hostile power
In Thy spirit, for the glory of the Father.
Amen.

Prayer from The Little Office of the Immaculate Conception of the Blessed Virgin Mary

Come, my lips, and wide proclaim,
The Blessed Virgin's spotless fame.

V. O Lady, make haste to befriend me.
R. From the hands of the enemy mightily defend me.

Glory be to the Father, and to the Son, and to the Holy Spirit.

As it was in the beginning, is now, and ever shall be, world without end. Amen. Alleluia.

Hymn

Hail Queen of the Heavens!
　Hail, Mistress of earth!
Hail, Virgin most pure,
　Of Immaculate birth!

Clear Star of the morning,
　In beauty enshrined!
O Lady, make speed
　To the help of mankind.

Thee God in the depth
   Of eternity chose;
And formed thee all fair
   As His glorious Spouse;

And called thee His Word's
   Own Mother to be,
By whom He created
   The earth, sky, and sea.

V. God elected her, and pre-elected her.
R. He made her to dwell in His tabernacle.

Let us Pray: O Holy Mary, Queen of Heaven, Mother of our Lord Jesus Christ, and Mistress of the world, who forsakest no one, and despisest no one; look upon me, O Lady, with an eye of pity, and entreat for me, of thy beloved Son, the forgiveness of all my sins; that, as I now celebrate with devout affection, thy holy and Immaculate Conception, (*and glorious Assumption and Coronation in Heaven*), so hereafter, I may receive the prize of eternal blessedness by the grace of Him, Whom thou, in virginity didst bring forth, Jesus Christ our Lord, Who with the Father and the Holy Spirit, liveth and reigneth in perfect Trinity, God, world without end. Amen.

V. O Lady, hear my prayer;
R. And let my cry come unto thee.

V. Let us bless the Lord.
R. Thanks be to God.

May the souls of the faithful departed through the mercy of God rest in peace. Amen.

V. O Lady, make haste to befriend me.
R. From the hands of the enemy mightily defend me.

Glory be to the Father, etc. Alleluia.

Hymn

Hail, Virgin most wise!
   Hail Deity's shrine!
With seven fair pillars.
   And table divine!

Preserved from the guilt
   Which hath come on us all!
Exempt, in the womb,
   From the taint of the fall.

O new star of Jacob!
   Of Angels, the Queen!

O gate of the Saints!
  O Mother of men!

O terrible as
  An embattled array
Be thou of the faithful
  The refuge and stay.

V. The Lord Himself created her in the Holy Ghost.
R. And poured her out among all His Works.

V. O Lady, hear my prayer;
R. And let my cry come unto thee.

Let us pray: O Holy Mary, Queen of, etc.

V. O Lady, hear my prayer;
R. And let my cry come unto thee.

V. Let us bless the Lord.
R. Thanks be to God.

May the souls of the faithful departed through the mercy of God rest in peace. Amen.

V. O Lady, make haste to befriend me.
R. From the hands of the enemy mightily defend me.

Glory be to the Father, etc. Alleluia.

Hymn

Hail, Solomon's throne!
  Pure ark of the law!
Fair rainbow! and bush
  Which the Patriarch saw!

Hail, Gedeon's fleece!
  Hail blossoming rod!
Samson's sweet honeycomb!
  Portal of God!

Well fitting it was,
  That a Son so divine
Should preserve from all touch
  Of original sin.

Nor suffer by smallest
  Defect to be stained,
That Mother, whom He
  For Himself, had ordained.

V. I dwell in the highest.
R. And my throne is on the pillar of the clouds.

V. O Lady, hear my prayer;
R. And let my cry come unto thee.

Let us pray: O Holy Mary, Queen of, etc.

V. O Lady, hear my prayer;
R. And let my cry come unto thee.

V. Let us bless the Lord.
R. Thanks be to God.

May the souls of the faithful departed through the mercy of God rest in peace. Amen.

V. O Lady, make haste to befriend me.
R. From the hands of the enemy mightily defend me.

Glory be to the Father, etc. Alleluia.

Hymn

Hail, Virginal Mother!
    Hail, purity's cell!
Fair shrine where the Trinity
    Loveth to dwell!

Hail, garden of pleasure!
    Celestial balm!
Cedar of chastity!
    Martyrdom's palm!

Thou land set apart
    From uses profane!
And free from the curse
    Which in Adam began!

Thou city of God!
  Thou gate of the East!
In Thee is all grace,
  O joy of the blest!

V. As the lily among the thorns;
R. So is my beloved among the daughters of Adam.

V. O Lady, hear my prayer;
R. And let my cry come unto thee.

Let us pray: O Holy Mary, Queen of, etc.

V. O Lady, hear my prayer;
R. And let my cry come unto thee.

V. Let us bless the Lord.
R. Thanks be to God.

May the souls of the faithful departed through the mercy of God rest in peace. Amen.

V. O Lady, make haste to befriend me.
R. From the hands of the enemy mightily defend me.

Glory be to the Father, etc. Alleluia.

Hymn

Hail, city of refuge!
  Hail, David's high tower!

With battlements crowned
  And girded with power!

Filled at thy conception
  With love and with light!
The dragon by thee
  Was shorn of his might!

O Woman most valiant!
  O Judith, thrice blessed!
As David was nursed
  At his fair mother's breast.

As the savior of Egypt
  Upon Rachel's knee,
So the world's great Redeemer,
  Was cherished by thee.

V. Thou art all fair, my beloved,
R. And the original stain was never in thee.

V. O Lady, hear my prayer;
R. And let my cry come unto thee.

Let us pray: O Holy Mary, Queen of, etc.

V. O Lady, hear my prayer;
R. And let my cry come unto thee.

V. Let us bless the Lord.
R. Thanks be to God.

May the souls of the faithful departed through the mercy of God rest in peace. Amen.

V. O Lady, make haste to befriend me.
R. From the hands of the enemy mightily defend me.

Glory be to the Father, etc. Alleluia.

Hymn

Hail, dial of Achaz!
   On thee the true Sun,
Told backward the course
   Which from old He had run!

And, that Man might be raised
   Submitting to shame,
A little more low
   Than the angels became.

Thou wrapt in the blaze
   Of His Infinite light,
Dost shine as the morn
   On the confines of night.

As the moon on the lost
   Through obscurity dawns;
The serpent's destroyer!
   A lily 'mid thorns!

V. I made an unfailing light to arise in heaven.
R. And as a mist I overspread the whole earth.

V. O Lady, hear my prayer;
R. And let my cry come unto thee.

Let us pray: O Holy Mary, Queen of, etc.

V. O Lady, hear my prayer;
R. And let my cry come unto thee.

V. Let us bless the Lord.
R. Thanks be to God.

May the souls of the faithful departed through the mercy of God rest in peace. Amen.

V. May Jesus Christ thy Son, reconciled by thy prayers, O Lady, convert our hearts.
R. And turn away His anger from us.

V. O Lady, make haste to befriend me.
R. From the hands of the enemy mightily defend me.

Glory be to the Father, etc. Alleluia.

Hymn

Hail, Mother most pure!
   Hail, Virgin renowned!

Hail, Queen with the stars
   As a diadem crowned!

Above all the angels
   In glory untold,
Standing next to the King
   In a vesture of gold!

O Mother of mercy!
   O star of the wave!
O hope of the guilty!
   O light of the grave!

Through thee may we come
   To the haven of rest;
And see heaven's King
   In the courts of the blest!

V. Thy name, O Mary, is as oil poured out.
R. Thy servants have loved thee exceedingly.

V. O Lady, hear my prayer;
R. And let my cry come unto thee.

Let us pray: O Holy Mary, Queen of, etc.

V. O Lady, hear my prayer;
R. And let my cry come unto thee.

V. Let us bless the Lord.
R. Thanks be to God.

May the souls of the faithful departed through the mercy of God rest in peace. Amen.

Terminate the Office as follows:

> These praises and prayers
>   I lay at thy feet,
> O Virgin of virgins!
>   O Mary most sweet!
>
> Be thou my true guide
>   Through this pilgrimage here;
> And stand by my side
>   When death draweth near.

Ant. This is the admirable Virgin who has contracted neither original sin, nor the least actual sin.

V. Thou hast been conceived without sin, O Holy Virgin.
R. Pray for us to God the Father whose Son thou hast brought forth.

Prayer

O God, who in preserving the most Holy Virgin from the stain of original sin hast prepared for Thy Son a worthy dwelling in the womb of this Immaculate Virgin, we beseech Thee, that as Thou hast preserved her from all sin by the anticipated merits of the death of this same Son, Thou wouldst also vouchsafe her intercession, to give us grace to arrive at the possession of Thee, purified from all our sins. Through Jesus Christ our Lord. Amen.

Say the Memorare

THE NEW SECRET OF SALVATION

Fatima and the Three Little Shepherds

Among the many Apparitions of Our Lady, memorable is the mysterious event that occurred at Fatima, in Portugal, the war-year 1917. The Blessed Virgin appeared to three innocent shepherds near Cova da Iria; they were Lucy, ten years old, and her two cousins, Francisco and Jacinta Marto, the former nine, the latter seven years of age.

Soon the smaller ones passed to eternal life, while Lucy, a few years after the apparitions entered the convent of St. Dorothy at Tuy in Spain, where, on the 3rd of October, 1928, she was named Sister Mary Lucy of the Sorrowful Mother.

In 1948, Sister Lucy left the Convent of the Sisters of St. Dorothy and entered a Carmelite Convent in Portugal.

The Blessed Virgin came on earth to bring a message from her Divine Son, to warn the world of present and future evils, to entrust to us a great secret with the promise of peace if the Rosary be recited, and the devotion to the Immaculate Heart of Mary be spread throughout the world.

Let us hear with gratitude and filial affection the touching and impressive words of Our Lady of Fatima.

First Apparition

Here is the first message: "I have come to ask you that you return here six times, at the same hour, the 13th of the month, and in October I shall tell you who I am and what I demand from you. Offer yourselves to God, practice self-denial, accept willingly all the trials He will send to you in reparation for the sins against the Divine Majesty; do this for the conversion of sinners and also to amend for all blasphemies and offenses made to the Immaculate Heart of Mary."

Second Apparition

It was the feast of St. Anthony; the three little shepherds together with other people had gathered at the same place, and had devoutly said the Rosary, when the beautiful Lady appeared saying: "Recite the Rosary every day, and after the "Glory" of each decade add this prayer: 'O my Jesus, pardon our sins, deliver us from the fire of Hell, give rest to the souls in Purgatory, especially to the most abandoned.'"

Then she told Lucy: "I shall come soon to take Jacinta and Francisco with me. You will remain on earth much longer, for Jesus wishes you to establish in the world the devotion to my Immaculate Heart." Then to each child she confided a secret, forbidding them, however, to reveal it to anyone.

Third Apparition—July 13th

The news of the apparition of Our Lady began to spread. On the 13th of July more than 5,000 people had gathered near Cova da Iria.

The White Lady appeared and recommended:

"Say the Rosary every day; say it frequently so that the war might end, because only the intercession of the Virgin could obtain this favor for suffering humanity. Continue to come here every month, and on the 13th of October I shall tell you who I am and what I desire. A miracle will occur so that the world will believe in my apparitions."

Apparitions of August and September

Lucy told the 30,000 people who had gathered: "You must pray." The Vision appeared, saying: "Persevere in reciting the Rosary, if you wish to see the end of the war. Pray hard and make sacrifices for the conversion of sinners. Know that many souls go to Hell because there is no one who is willing to sacrifice himself for them."

Last Apparition
The Long Expected Message

The crowd was immense: 70,000 people waiting to see what would happen. The deaf, dumb, blind and crippled were praying for a miracle to happen that would set them free from their ailments. Lo and behold! the divine Vision appeared again, and Lucy, in order to obey the Ecclesiastical Authorities, exclaimed: "Who are you, and what do you want?" The Vision answered: "*I AM THE LADY OF THE ROSARY*, and demand that a shrine be erected here in my honor. I have come to plead with all the faithful to amend their lives, to beg pardon for their sins and to resolve never to offend the Lord again. Continue to say the Rosary every day. I promise that, if men will change their sinful life I will answer their prayers, and the war will end soon."

Frightful Vision

In a rapid vision, the Virgin made the three innocent children see Hell, where thousands of sinful souls fall every day. Frightened, the children looked at Mary ... who, with sorrowful accent, said: "In order to save the sinners, the Lord wishes to establish in the world the devotion to my Immaculate Heart. If what I tell you will be done, many souls will be saved, and there will be peace; but, if it is not done, Divine Justice will demand new and heavier punishments. The present war (1914-1918) is about to end, but if men do not cease to offend God, in a short time, during the next Pontificate (of Pius XI) another war, worse than this, will start. (It was the second world war.)

"When a night shall be brightened by a strange light, know that it is the sign God gives you to warn the world that the punishment for its crimes is near. There will be war, famine, and persecution against the Church and the Holy Father. In order to prevent this, I urge the consecration of the world to my Immaculate Heart, and the Communion of Reparation every first Saturday of the month.

"If what I demand will be done, Russia will be converted, and there will be peace, otherwise (as sadly happened) grave errors will spread through the world and will cause more wars and persecutions against the Church; many good Christians will suffer martyrdom, and the Holy Father will suffer greatly; several nations will be destroyed, but in the end, my Immaculate Heart will be triumphant! The Holy Father will consecrate Russia to me, and humanity will have an era of peace."

Perpetual Novena in honor of Our Lady of the Miraculous Medal

Lourdes Hymn

Immaculate Mary,
 thy praises we sing,
Who reignest in splendor
 With Jesus, our King.

Chorus
Ave, Ave, Ave, Maria!
 Ave, Ave, Maria!

Thy name is our power,
 thy virtues our light,
Thy love is our comfort,
 thy pleading our light.

Chorus

Reading of Announcements and Favors

Opening Prayer

Priest: In the name of the Father and of the Son, and of the Holy Spirit.

People: Amen.

Priest: Come O Holy Spirit, fill the hearts of Your faithful, and kindle in them the fire of Your love.
Send forth Your Spirit, and they shall be created.

People: And You shall renew the face of the earth.

Priest: Let us pray.
O God, who did instruct the hearts of the faithful by the light of the Holy Spirit, grant us in the same Spirit to be truly wise and ever to rejoice in His consolation, through Jesus Christ our Lord.

People: Amen.

Priest: O Mary, conceived without sin,

People: Pray for us who have recourse to you. (3 times)

Priest and People: O Lord Jesus Christ, who have vouchsafed to glorify by numberless miracles the Blessed Virgin Mary, immaculate from the first moment of her conception, grant that all who devoutly implore her protection on earth, may eternally enjoy Your Presence in heaven, who, with the Father and Holy Spirit, live and reign, God for ever and ever. Amen.

O Lord Jesus Christ, who for the accomplishment of Thy greatest works, have chosen the weak things of the world, that no flesh may glory in Thy sight; and who for a better and more widely diffused belief in the Immaculate Conception of Thy Mother, have wished that the Miraculous Medal be manifested to Saint Catherine Laboure, grant, we beseech Thee, that filled with like humility, we may glorify this mystery by word and work. Amen.

Memorare

Priest and People: Remember, O most compassionate Virgin Mary, that never was it known that anyone who fled to thy protection, implored thy assistance, or sought thy intercession, was left unaided. Inspired with this confidence, we fly unto thee, O Virgin of virgins, our Mother; to thee we come; before thee we kneel sinful and sorrowful. O Mother of the Word Incarnate, despise not our petitions, but in thy clemency hear and answer them. Amen.

Novena Prayer

Priest and People: O Immaculate Virgin Mary, Mother of Our Lord Jesus and our Mother, penetrated with the most lively confidence in your all-powerful and never-failing intercession, manifested so often through the Miraculous Medal, we your loving and trustful children implore you to obtain for us the graces and favors we ask during this Novena, if they be beneficial to our immortal souls, and the souls for whom we pray. (*Here privately form your petitions.*) You know, O Mary, how often our souls have been the sanctuaries of your Son who hates iniquity. Obtain for us then a deep hatred of sin and that purity of heart which will attach us to God alone so that our every thought, word and deed may tend to His greater glory. Obtain for us also a spirit of prayer and self-denial that we may recover by penance what we have lost by sin and at length attain to that blessed abode where you are the Queen of angels and of men. Amen.

An Act of Consecration to Our Lady of the Miraculous Medal

Priest and People: O Virgin Mother of God, Mary Immaculate, we dedicate and consecrate ourselves to you under the title of Our Lady of the Miraculous Medal. May this Medal be for each one of us a sure sign of your affection for us and a constant reminder of our duties toward you. Ever while wearing it, may we be blessed by your loving protection and preserved in the grace of your Son. O most powerful Virgin, Mother of our Savior, keep us close to you every moment of our lives. Obtain for us, your children, the grace of a happy death; so that, in union with you, we may enjoy the bliss of heaven forever. Amen.

Priest: O Mary conceived without sin.

People: Pray for us who have recourse to thee. (3 times)

Short Sermon

Benediction of the Most Blessed Sacrament

(Note: Diocesan regulations may dictate the use of another translation)

Humbly let us voice our homage
    For so great a sacrament,
Let all former rites surrender
    To the Lord's New Testament;
What our senses fail to fathom
    Let us grasp through faith's consent!
Glory, honor, adoration
    Let us sing with one accord!
Praised be God, almighty Father;
    Praised be Christ, His Son, Our Lord;
Praised be God the Holy Spirit;
    Triune Godhead be adored! Amen.

Let us Pray

Priest: God, who left us in this wondrous sacrament a memorial of Your Passion, help us, we beg You, so to reverence the sacred mysteries of Your Body and Blood, that we may always experience the effects of Your Redemption. Who live and reign forever and ever.

People: Amen.

Hymn
Hail, Holy Queen Enthroned Above
(All seated)

Hail, holy Queen enthroned above,
  O Maria.
Hail, Queen of mercy and of love,
  O Maria.

Chorus
  Triumph, all ye Cherubim,
  Sing with us, ye Seraphim,
  Heav'n and earth resound the hymn:
  Salve, Salve, Salve Regina.

The cause of joy to men below,
  O Maria.
The spring through which all graces flow,
  O Maria.

Chorus

O gentle, loving, holy one,
  O Maria.
The God of Light became your Son,
  O Maria.

Chorus

The Divine Praises

Blessed be God.
Blessed be His holy Name.
Blessed be Jesus Christ, true God and true Man.
Blessed be the Name of Jesus.
Blessed be His Most Sacred Heart.
Blessed be His Most Precious Blood.
Blessed be Jesus in the most holy Sacrament of the Altar.
Blessed be the Holy Spirit, the Paraclete.
Blessed be the great Mother of God, Mary most holy.
Blessed be her holy and Immaculate Conception.
Blessed be her glorious Assumption.
Blessed be the name of Mary, Virgin and Mother.
Blessed be St. Joseph, her most chaste spouse.
Blessed be God in His angels and in His saints.

May the Heart of Jesus, in the Most Blessed Sacrament, be praised, adored and loved, with grateful affection, at every moment, in all the tabernacles of the world, even to the end of time. Amen.

Sing: *O Mary, conceived without sin,*
Pray for us, pray for us.
O Mary, conceived without sin,
Pray for us who have recourse to thee.

ST PAULS

This book was produced by St. Pauls/Alba House, the Society of St. Paul, an international religious congregation of priests and brothers dedicated to serving the Church through the communications media.

For information regarding this and associated ministries of the Pauline Family of Congregations, write to the Vocation Director, Society of St. Paul, P.O. Box 189, 9531 Akron-Canfield Road, Canfield, Ohio 44406-0189. Phone (330) 702-0359; or E-mail: spvocationoffice@aol.com or check our internet site, www.albahouse.org